Tarantulas

Leo Statts

Kaeden.com
KaedenBooks.com
(800) 890-7323

Published by Kaeden Books™, PO Box 16190, Rocky River, Ohio 44116. Kaeden Books™ is a trademark of Kaeden Corporation. Copyright © 2017 by Kaeden Corporation. Kaeden Focus Library™ and FOCUS ON™ are trademarks of Kaeden Corporation. This edition is published under license from ABDO Publishing Company, Inc. ABDO™ is a trademark of ABDO Publishing Company, Inc.

ISBN: 978-1-63584-023-0 (paperback)

Title: FOCUS ON Animals: Tarantulas
Author: Leo Statts
Editor: Brienna Rossiter
Series Designer: Madeline Berger
Art Direction: Dorothy Toth

Printed in Guangzhou, China
NOR/0117/CA21602021

First edition: 2017

Table of Contents

Tarantulas

Tarantulas are spiders.
Some people keep them as pets.

Some are tiny. Others can be as big as dinner plates.

Body

Tarantulas have eight legs. They are covered in hair. Most tarantulas are black or brown. Some are very colorful.

Tarantulas have **fangs**.

They use their fangs to dig holes or bite prey.

Habitat

Tarantulas live in many places. Most live in **deserts** and **grasslands**. Some live in **rain forests**.

■ Where tarantulas live

Some tarantulas live in trees.
Some live under rocks or leaves.

Others dig holes
in the ground.

Food

Tarantulas eat insects.
They eat other spiders.
Some eat mice and birds, too.

Tarantulas hide. They wait for prey. Then they jump out and bite. **Venom** in their fangs helps kill the prey.

Life Cycle

Tarantulas lay hundreds of eggs at a time. Baby spiders are called spiderlings.

Tarantulas can live up to 30 years in the wild.

Average Size

A tarantula is smaller than a basketball.

7.75 in

9.5 in

Average Weight

A tarantula is heavier than a quarter.

0.14 lbs

0.01 lbs

Glossary

desert - a very dry, sandy area with little plant growth

fangs - long, narrow teeth

grassland - a large area of grass, with few or no trees

prey - an animal that is hunted and eaten by another animal

rain forest - a tropical woodland where it rains a lot

venom - a poison in the bite or sting of some animals

Index

BOOKS IN THIS SERIES

Alligators

Camels

Caribou

Cheetahs

Cobras (July 2017)

Dragonflies (July 2017)

Elephants

Giraffes (July 2017)

Iguanas

Komodo Dragons

Orangutans (July 2017)

Penguins (July 2017)

Polar Bears (July 2017)

Salamander (July 2017)

Seals (July 2017)

Tarantulas

Tigers (July 2017)

Toucans